French: Lion

English: Lion

Arabic : أسد

French: éléphant

English: elephant

Arabic : فيل

French: chien

English: dog

Arabic : كلب

French: cheval

English: horse

Arabic : حصان

French: chat

English: cat

Arabic : قطة

French: gorille

English: gorilla

Arabic : غوريلا

French: lapin

English: rabbit

Arabic : أرنب

French: mouton

English: sheep

Arabic : خروف

French: poulet

English: chicken

Arabic : دجاجة

French: tortue

English: turtle

Arabic : سلحفاة

French: girafe

English: giraffe

Arabic : زرافة

French: vache

English: cow

Arabic : بقرة

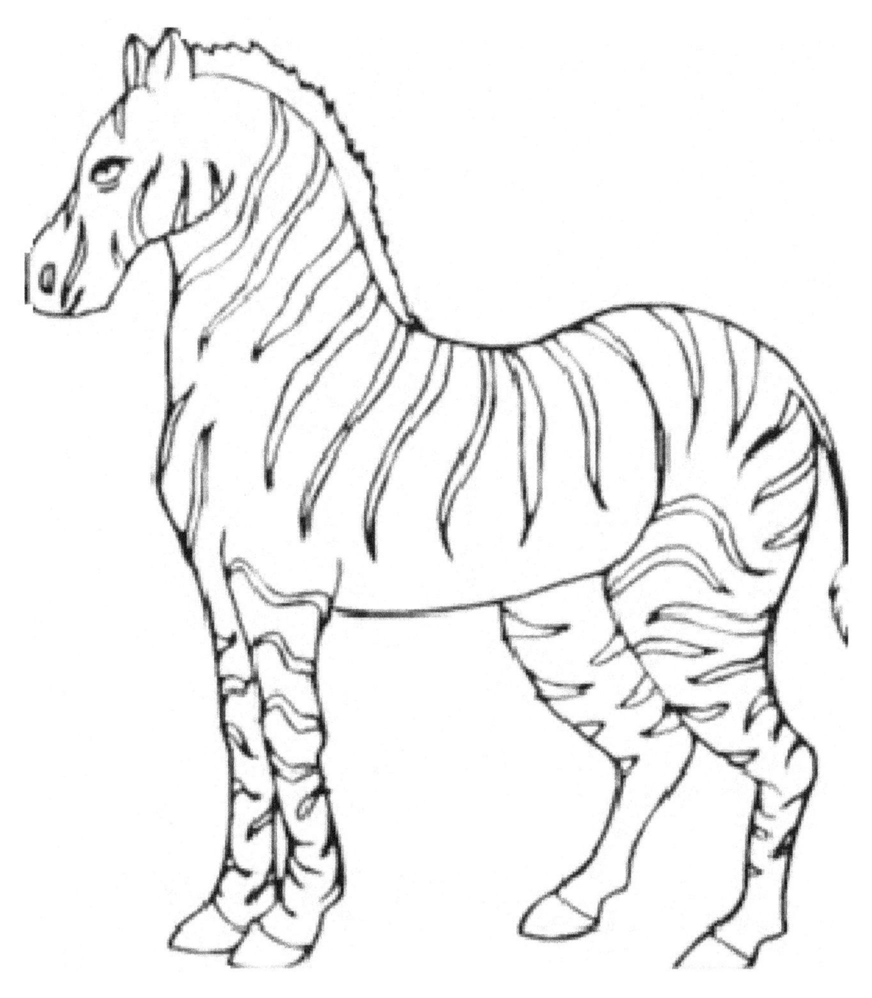

French: zèbre

English: zebra

Arabic : حمار وحشي

French: aigle

English: eagle

Arabic : نسر

French: ver de terre

English: earthworm

Arabic : دودة

French: cochon

English: pig

Arabic : خنزير

French: singe

English: monkey

Arabic : قرد

French: dauphin

English: dolphin

Arabic : دلفين

French: canard

English: duck

Arabic : بطة

French: souris

English: mouse

Arabic : فأر

French: poulpe

English: octopus

Arabic : أخطبوط

French: poisson

English: fish

Arabic : سمكة

French: serpent

English: snake

Arabic : ثعبان

French: loup

English: wolf

Arabic : ذئب

French: chameau

English: camel

Arabic : جمل

French: hippopotame

English: hippopotamus

Arabic : فرس النهر

French: papillon

English: butterfly

Arabic : فراشة

French: abeille

English: bee

Arabic : نحلة

French: oiseau

English : bird

Arabic : عصفورة

French: cerf

English: deer

Arabic : غزالة

French: grenouille

English: frog

Arabic : ضفدع

French: crocodile

English: crocodile

Arabic : تمساح

French: tigre

English: tiger

Arabic : نمر

French: ours

English: bear

Arabic : دب

French: kangourou

English: kangaroo

Arabic : كنغر

French: renard

English: fox

Arabic : ثعلب